Dedication

To my sweet Brayden and all the babies never born, born with their eyes closed, lived a brief life, or never made it to adulthood. This book is for you and how you changed our hearts and lives. You will never be forgotten. Brayden, you left an enormous footprint on my heart, even with the smallest feet.

To the moms of these special babies, find your joy again.

Brayden's precious footprint

reminds me of Jeremiah 1:5,

"I knew you before I formed you

in your mother's womb."

BY KINDRA KING

Moms of Morning

FINDING JOY AFTER A SEASON OF GRIEF

Moms of Morning
Finding Joy After a Season of Grief
Copyright © 2022 Kindra King

Scriptures marked KJV are taken from the KING JAMES VERSION (KJV): KING JAMES VERSION, public domain.

Scriptures marked NIV are taken from the NEW INTERNATIONAL VERSION (NIV): Scripture taken from THE HOLY BIBLE, NEW INTERNATIONAL VERSION ®. Copyright © 1973, 1978, 1984, 2011 by Biblica, Inc.™. Used by permission of Zondervan

Publisher: SpeakTruth Media Group, LLC
PO Box 1448, Crockett TX 75835-7448

Book design by SpeakTruth Media Group, LLC.

ISBN: 979-8-9857296-2-7 *(pb)*
         979-8-9857296-3-4 *(hc)*

Printed in the USA

Acknowledgments

To my Dad, that gave me the idea to start writing this book in the first place after sharing my dream with you. You have said for so long that others needed to hear my story, and here it is. You have encouraged me each step of this process and have often called telling me that you needed my book for someone you've known who has suffered this type of loss. Thank you doesn't seem adequate, Dad. Thank you for believing in me always. Thank you for lifting me on days that I have been down. Thank you for taking Justin under your wing and planning Brayden's funeral. Thank you for jumping on a plane twenty years ago to be with us. But most of all, thank you for your prayers. They have sustained me so many times in my life. I am so blessed to call you Dad. I love you!

To my husband, Justin, what a journey we have been on. I would never have wanted to do this thing called life with anyone else. Losing our precious son was the hardest thing we have ever done, and what satan tried to use as evil, God turned into good. It wasn't always the smoothest of roads, but we made it. I am so proud of the man you are and where you have allowed God to take you in your life. Thank you for giving me the gift of being a mother. Thank you for showering me with grace, forgiveness, love, and support. You have always been my biggest supporter in everything I have ever desired to do, including writing this book. Thank you for pushing me! Thank you for never giving up! Thank you for sitting with me many nights and wiping the tears from my face. Always know I am your biggest supporter and fan. I love you the mostest!

To my beautiful Rainbow baby Destiny, words cannot express how wonderful you are to me or proud you make me every day. I have said many times that "if you were not my child, I would still want to know you." It has been such an honor being your mama, a title and name I have never taken lightly. Thank you for allowing me to share Brayden with you and loving him like you do. Thank you for listening a

hundred times to this book and getting emotional with me each time. I am grateful for the mosquito bites we received after having a deep conversation on the porch about this book and life in general. Destiny, you saved me. I know that I have made many mistakes as a mom but know that I have always loved you with every ounce of my body. I would sit on bed rest for twelve weeks again to know you. You are the rainbow I needed after a massive storm. I love you, Sissymomma!

Mom, thank you for always uplifting me in my life. You have been my pillar of strength. Thank you for the hours of prayer for Justin and me. Thank you for opening your home after Brayden passed, and I did not have to go back to that house. Thank you for nursing me back to health after surgery.

This book is for moms and Nanas who don't know what to do for their babies. Thank you for climbing into bed with me many nights and holding me so I could just cry. Sometimes in those silent moments was when the loudest emotions were spoken. Tears indeed are a language only God understands. So many tears. Thank you for NEVER forgetting Brayden's birthday and always calling to see how we are. I love you, Mom, and would never have made it through all this without you.

Redge, you know what you have done. I could never thank you enough for all you do and your belief in me. I love you dearly!

To my nurses, my angels, Paula, Tonia, Sue, Pat, Sam, and Bennie. I can never thank or repay you for everything you did for me, Brayden, Justin, and Destiny. You inspire me to be a nurse like each of you were to me and uplift women in their most vulnerable times. I love each of you so very much!

To Dr. Davis, thank you for going above and beyond for your patients. You were a God send to me, and I appreciate all the tears, prayers, and support you gave me during my pregnancies. You have a special place in my heart, always!

To my family and friends that have been unwavering in your love and support for me through this journey, I love you!

To all the beautiful moms, thank you for being a part of my journey. I pray that my story can uplift you. I pray that you can begin to share your story. I pray that one day I can meet and hug your neck. I pray that my story can help you start healing, as much as it was healing for me to write this book. Always know you are never alone! God bless each of you, and I pray you find joy in the morning.

Last but certainly not least, to my Brayden, my angel, my champ. Here is our story—my journey of pain, my story, and my way back to joy because of you. You changed my life for the better. I dream of you and who you would be. I loved you from the moment I knew you were growing inside me. You made a significant footprint on my heart, even with little feet.

I look forward to holding you in my arms one day and never letting you go. I am so blessed to be your mommy!

Praise for
Moms of Morning

"MOM: 'Moms of Morning,' I absolutely love this book! It touches on topics that can be difficult for people to talk about. The author allows the reader to experience the many emotions throughout the book. This book brings light and hope to the brokenhearted." — Adrian Patton

"A must-read for any mom that has experienced the trauma of losing a child or the inability to have children. Kindra takes you through the real-life experience of love, hope, traumatic loss, and the journey out of loss, back into hope, and love again. Through her powerful personal testimony, she empowers moms of mourning to understand the loss with love, embrace pain with peace, and look to the future with faith. Her openness and transparency transcend the taboo nature and stigma our culture has placed on premature child loss. A long-needed and awaited personal conversation the world of moms has longed for." — Shana Guillotte

"'Moms of Morning' is a beautiful, raw, and honest story that captures this mama's reality while helping all other mothers or families in mourning. It is a short read that quickly grabs your attention but also fulfills its purpose in the 45-60 minutes you take to read it. You will take away a great message and learn.

As a hospice nurse, I found her book to be very helpful to assist any grieving mother that I have the honor and privilege to support in her child's care. I believe 'Moms of Morning' is needed in places like hospitals, hospices, counselor's offices, and funeral homes for grieving mothers that feel alone in this world.

All in all, a great book with a powerful message." — Britnee Gandhi

Contents

Introduction

His name was chosen, his nursery
painted, and the bond between mother and
son formed. No one told me to anticipate
planning a funeral or what to expect after
suffering the most tremendous loss of my life.
I was twenty-one years old, newly married,
and my life spun out of control with grief. I
left the hospital with an open wound and a
memory box filled with items that belonged to
my son in his short life. Not knowing what
the future was going to look like after this. I

was uncertain if I would be the same again, and I was not.

I was surrounded by family and friends but felt utterly alone. In my hometown, no grief center or counseling was offered to moms who experienced the loss of an infant/baby. Losing a child can still be a taboo subject for people to talk about. No one speaks about such a hard experience. When a spouse loses their partner, they are called widows or widowers. When a child loses their parent, they are called orphans. It is simply against the natural order for a parent to bury their child.

The grief journey is different for everyone. After enduring this loss, I fought with faith, blamed my body for betraying me, and struggled to understand my husband's emotions. No one could or did prepare me for the dark days after my son's death. I questioned my faith in a way I had never before.

I wanted to help others like me. I desired to use my testimony to help families going through the loss I endured. I needed people to be aware of what women face internally after losing their children. But also, to help them understand that this burden does not have to be faced alone and that others are going through what you are. Grief is tricky in how and when it will hit you, even years later.

I strived to help people like myself but wanted to reach many more. I dreamt about a tree with a butterfly, and that butterfly had Brayden's name on it. I spoke to my dad about it, and he suggested I try to write my story down. That night, I dreamt of the same tree, but instead of one butterfly, there were thousands of them, each representing a loss. It took a dream, a conversation, and twenty years to prepare my heart to share my story with the world. I realized that other moms might need to hear what I had to share, the wisdom I learned through this grief journey, and the courage to wake up each day and keep moving forward. New grace is given each morning, and joy is ours to have again.

I wrote this book hoping to reach every person who has experienced the loss of a child. I want you to understand better the grief and struggles you face and, eventually, the joy that comes from the long journey you endure.

I hope that this book can be the stepping stone to your healing. I pray that my story will bless you as it blesses me to share it with each of you. Thank you for allowing me to share my Brayden with you.

Excitement

Oh, my word, two minutes is a long time waiting for a line to appear on a stick you just peed on to discover if you are pregnant. I could not believe I was waiting for this plus sign to appear. I had not been married even six months. I married the love of my life Justin, my high school sweetheart, and we may be becoming parents. EEEK! So exciting!

Yep, that is a plus sign. I am pregnant. The absolute joy that filled my heart immediately was overwhelming. I wanted a baby for as long as I could remember, but I honestly never knew how much until that moment. We were elated! We, of course, did not wait until I was out of my first trimester to tell the world. We wanted everyone to know.

We found out when I was sixteen weeks pregnant that we would be welcoming a baby boy to our family. The planning of the nursery was underway. We wanted unique and fun, so we chose the Harley Davidson theme.

Now for the naming of this sweet boy. We could not agree on a name. We looked in so many "baby name" books. Until the day we heard the name Brayden, we both looked at each other and knew that was it! The name was perfect.

I sang, read books, and talked to Brayden daily. When Justin came home from work, he did the same thing. We were in complete awe of this sweet baby growing inside of me. We could not wait to hold him in our arms and watch him grow. We were utterly oblivious to the danger of pregnancy or what could be lurking. I had never known anyone that experienced a difficult pregnancy. I had heard of people miscarrying a child early but never after the first trimester. I was in a bubble of euphoria. Everything was perfect.

September is too Early

I was twenty-four weeks pregnant (six months) and was feeling amazing! I was finally over the morning sickness, and my crazy food cravings were behind me. I woke up on that September morning not feeling great. No pain or cramping, but Brayden had been highly active during the night, and I did not sleep well. It felt like he kept moving to one side of my stomach and would just stay there. As Justin left for work, I told him I would return to bed for a bit.

I laid there for over an hour before my pregnant bladder made me get up. I went into the bathroom and discovered I was bleeding—a lot! As many of you know, this is something no pregnant woman wants to experience. It is not normal, especially this far along.

I immediately called my doctor's office and was told to go straight to the hospital. I called Justin to ask him to meet me there. My mom came to pick me up. She worked at the hospital and was two blocks from where we lived at the time. A nurse took me immediately by wheelchair to the Labor and Delivery unit.

Upon arrival at the delivery unit, I was not examined right away. I was mistreated by one nurse in particular, who patronized me about my reaction to the bleeding. She made it a point to ask if I was a first-time mom. For lack of words, I was told I was overreacting and probably dehydrated. However, all of that was about to change. When she finally did a vaginal exam, her entire demeanor changed towards me. She told me not to get out of bed for any reason and that she would return shortly. She did just that with a second nurse in tow. She explained that the charge nurse would be doing an exam on me. When the second nurse finished, they gave each other a knowing look, and chaos of activity ensued. As I was put into Trendelenburg position, I asked, "What is happening?" That's when I learned I was "very dilated," ten centimeters to be exact. What does that mean? I had been in full labor and had not even known it.

My doctor arrived and explained that he thought I had an incompetent cervix, which means the cervix shortens in length and causes preterm dilation. He gave me steroids to help mature Brayden's lungs. Most people do not know about this condition because once the dilation has happened, contractions often start after. The night before, while I thought Brayden was moving around, I was actually having contractions that did not cause pain or cramping. I experienced a kind of labor that was not what I had seen in the movies, where the woman is screaming as soon as the first contraction starts. I was told they would do everything they could to keep Brayden safe and hopefully hold off on delivery, which meant I would be in the hospital until my due date if possible.

An amazing nurse came on duty that afternoon and explained all that could happen if I delivered that day. She told me Brayden would be extremely small and vulnerable to many horrible things that I was unprepared for. He could be blind, with some form of brain damage, cerebral palsy, susceptible to infection, and possibly suffer a heart attack or stroke. The list went on and on. She also stated that if he was born early, he might have translucent skin, and if he did, they would wrap him in a material like cling wrap to prevent him from losing too much body heat. So many things could go wrong. I was scared. Justin was scared. Our family was scared.

As I lay there for hours, afraid to move, our family gathered to be with us. We had many people surrounding us to show support. Around eight o'clock that evening, I looked at my husband with tears streaming down my face and told him I needed to push. Pushing was an internal feeling that I had never felt before but an automatic physical action I could not deny. We called for the nurse; it was time.

A Precious Cry

The medical staff wheeled me into a sterile room, it was cold and bright, and the smell of cleanser assaulted my senses. My entire body was shaking from the cold, or was it fear? My doctor scrubbed in, the NICU team was in place, and the drape was up, so I could not see what was happening. Brayden had turned into a breech position, so the decision that a cesarean section was the best course of action for delivery. I saw a gush of blood from above the drape when the incision was made and felt a severe amount of pressure. Then I heard the most precious little cry. It was a soft cry, so perfect. I was immediately filled with joy and flooded with a love I had never known. I was a mom! My baby Brayden cried! Hope soared through the room!

So many things were happening all at once. The NICU team was trying to make sure Brayden was stable for transport to a higher care facility. He was wrapped in what I call cling wrap to help ensure his body heat would not escape his fragile body. I was taken to a recovery room with my precious nurse by my side. She was even elated that he cried. She heard him too. In recovery, I was told that another devastating thing had happened during surgery. When the incision was made, my placenta was on top of my uterus, and it was cut through. Brayden and I had lost significant amounts of blood. We both were possibly going to need blood transfusions.

Before the NICU team left with Brayden, they wheeled him in to see me, Justin, and some of our family. I was unable to hold him because he was intubated. He had multiple IVs and tubes all over him. I touched his tiny arm and talked to him. When I spoke to him, he wiggled his tiny toes. He knew his mama's voice. All the pregnancy books had been correct about him knowing my voice if I talked to or read to him. I only spent a few precious and treasured moments with him.

Phone Calls

After such a long and emotionally charged day, our family started trickling out one by one. We decided that Justin would go to the other hospital with Brayden, and my sister would stay with me. The joy of becoming a mother was pure ecstasy! All the emotions that any mother has, I had! I was postpartum, and I received a phone call from the physician caring for Brayden. He told me that Brayden had made the transfer beautifully. No strokes, no heart attacks, the intubation machine was doing what it was supposed to do. BUT (I hate that word), his blood levels were critically low, and he needed a blood transfusion immediately. Again, I heard about all the possible risks. The blood could cause him to go blind, again brain damage, possible hemorrhage, or it could fix the problem and overcome one of many hurdles. The risk of giving it to him was significant, but not giving it to him meant death. Worst scenario ever!

I spoke to Justin, and we agreed to give the needed blood. We would do whatever was needed for Brayden. Justin assured me he would be right by Brayden's side the entire time. We consented to the blood, and the transfusion began.

Anyone that has ever received a phone call early in the morning hours knows it usually is never good news on the other end of the line. It was sometime after four a.m. when the hospital phone rang. I answered quickly, hoping for an update on my Brayden. Justin was on the other end of the line and could barely speak. He told me that Brayden was gone. His sweet little body was too fragile and hemorrhaged during the transfusion. I do not remember much after that moment. My sister said that I let out a cry and dropped the phone. Honestly, all I remember was the pain and feeling of helplessness. I remember thinking, why God? Why Brayden? What did I do? What did Justin do? I was a mom for eight hours, which is not long enough! We had plans! We have a lifetime to give to this sweet baby. Eight hours is all we get? Why God? Why? Why?

Picnic Baskets

The need to touch, hold, memorize, and smell Brayden was so intense after I knew he was gone. I had to see him. I needed to be near him. I wanted my baby! Because Brayden was transferred to another hospital, they could not "readmit" Brayden to where I was. I told my nurses and doctor that they had to get him to me. I needed this more than anything at that moment. The only way to make this happen was to call a funeral home so that they could bring Brayden to me.

The family gathered as word spread of Brayden passing. Justin stayed with Brayden until the hospital finished bathing him and the funeral home picked him up. He raced to be with me before Brayden arrived.

A stranger entered my room holding a picnic basket. I was so confused as to why anyone would send a picnic lunch to us during this time. I could not fathom it. Picnics are for sunny days at a park with your family. Picnics are happy and fun. I did not know that laying in that picnic basket was my perfect Brayden. He was so tiny he fit in a picnic basket.

Reality began to set in as the funeral director laid Brayden in my arms. He indeed was not here anymore. His little body looked perfect. He had brown wavy hair, eyelashes that would make any woman envious, a perfect button nose, and beautiful pouty lips.

He was not transparent, as I was warned he might be, being so premature. He had an olive complexion. I counted his fingers and toes like any other new mama. I kissed his sweet nose. He was beautiful and perfect. The most beautiful person I had ever seen in my life. He was just tiny! So very tiny.

I held him for what felt like a few minutes but was actually several hours. When I heard it was time for him to go, I thought, "How do you let your baby go? How do you let them go knowing this was the last time you would hold them in your arms?" I did not want to say goodbye. I did not know how to say goodbye. I wanted to hold him forever and memorize his every feature, so I would never forget his appearance. I wanted to breathe him in and remember everything.

The funeral director took my son, placed him back in the picnic basket, wiped tears from his eyes, and left with my son. I still cannot look at a picnic basket and not think of Brayden. My arms were empty, and my heart was broken. I had no idea what to do next.

Baby Blue Shoebox

The day of Brayden's funeral was a dark, dreary, and rainy day. It was fitting because that was exactly how I felt inside. I remember my mom asking me what I wanted to wear to the funeral. I told her I did not care. I had thought of the outfit I'd planned to wear on the day we brought Brayden home. Never a funeral outfit for my child. I broke down as I sat on my mom's bed while she braided my hair. I told my mom I did not want to do this. I did not want to go! I did not know how I was going to get through this day.

After arriving at the cemetery, I lingered in the car, realizing the finality of the moment, saying goodbye to my son. My son that I had loved from the moment that stick had a plus sign on it, the son that I loved when I did not even know he was a boy, the son I loved the first time I heard a heartbeat, the son I would have gladly laid my life down for so he could live the life we'd planned for him.

As I approached the graveside, I noticed a blue "box" surrounded by flowers. It surprised me. I had no part in planning the funeral because I was still in the hospital recovering from major surgery. Justin and my dad planned it all. I had no idea caskets even came that small. I had no idea I was looking at a casket. It looked like a baby blue shoe box. The exact shade of blue we had chosen for his nursery.

Inside that "shoe box" was Brayden wrapped in the first thing I bought after finding out I was pregnant, a yellow blanket with the words "You are my sunshine" on it. He also wore a crocheted onesie that volunteers at the hospital make for babies who were tiny like him.

I hated the finality of saying "goodbye" to Brayden and leaving him. His little life had just begun, and now it was over.

Dark Days

I realized days and weeks after losing Brayden that I was not okay. I was broken with a gaping wound on my stomach, but no baby. I had all the after-pregnancy hormones but no baby. I had a threatening milk supply but no baby. I felt like sleeping all day, which helped me escape some of the pain. I wanted to overmedicate on the pain pills given for the c-section to help me stay asleep. I cannot say I was suicidal. I wanted to be numb for a while.

As with any death, the family leaves and goes back to their lives. Frequent phone calls stop after a few weeks. Loneliness crept up on me. I had no idea what I was supposed to do now. That is when I got angry.

I was angry about everything. I was mad at myself, my family, and my friends but mostly at God. I could not fathom that a God who was so good and loved me would take my child. I was mad that God created women to do what I was trying to do, have a baby, and would not "allow" my body to give birth correctly! Why in the world could I not carry a baby to term? How could I not have known that I was in labor? My OWN body betrayed me! My body was created for childbirth. I am a woman; I am supposed to be able to carry a child! What was wrong with me?

So, I cried! I cried all the time. I would see an insurance commercial and cry because a happy family with a new baby saved money switching to GEICO. Mom told me one day, "Tears are a language only God can understand." Wow, I was communicating to God a lot with this type of language! I wanted no part of it. I refused to go to church. I wanted nothing to do with Him. I was so angry with God, yet I cried out to Him daily! I was yelling, cursing, and felt so betrayed by Him.

Don't Say Anything

The fact is that people do not know what to say during times of loss. Losing an elderly person who has lived a long life is entirely different from losing a pregnancy that barely had time to start, a baby that is stillborn, or a baby that lived eight hours or eight years. I had to learn to give grace over time to people who do not know what to say.

Here is the biggest secret: *you do not have to say anything.* You can simply be a comfort by being present.

One of the hard things I was asked was, "If you knew it would turn out this way would you do it again?" Umm, yes, I would! I would not know what it was to be a mom without Brayden. Of course, I would do it again, to see his face and hear that cry! Would I hope to have the knowledge I do now, so I could prevent it from happening? Yes! Two completely different things.

And please do not tell me you know exactly how I feel. No, you do not! You do not because Brayden was not your son. Just as many of you are reading this book, I do not know how you feel because it is your loss. I can empathize with you, understand loss, and relate to your loss, but it is YOUR loss. It is YOUR child!

It is okay to question God. Even Jesus asked God before he went to the cross. In Matthew 26:39, the Scripture says, *"And he went a little farther, and fell on his face, and prayed, saying, O my Father, if it be possible,* **let this cup pass from me***: nevertheless, not as I will, but as thou wilt"* (KJV). That's a question. Why, Father, do I have to do this? Can you please find another way? Why me, Father?

I do not believe that anyone ever said anything to hurt me maliciously. People genuinely want to ease the pain, or at least try. It is hard to understand the magnitude of losing a child unless you have experienced the loss yourself. I believe that people were only trying to help and comfort me during that time, but I was angry with God, so to hear that He would not give me more than I could handle was difficult to understand. 2 Corinthians 12:9 states, *"My grace is sufficient for thee: for strength is made perfect in weakness."* (KJV). If you do not know what to say, "I am sorry" truly is enough and okay. Calling to check on a grieving mom or getting her out of the house for coffee, just being a comfort to her, helps so much. Understand this, moms, their intentions are good, but sometimes our pain is so overwhelming that we become easily offended. Know that they love you and desperately want to find a way to help you through this difficult time.

All the Grief Stages

Most of us have heard of the grief stages: denial, anger, bargaining, depression, and acceptance. It feels like I have gone through the stages of grief about a million times. Denial, he is not gone—anger, why my baby. Bargaining, God take me, spare him. Depression, days of sleeping, self-medicating, loathing myself. Acceptance is still a work in progress.

Grief strikes at the oddest moments. When you think you have moved on to the next stage of grief, you take two steps back. It may be because you struggle with fertility, but a friend who was not even trying to get pregnant gets pregnant because she took an antibiotic while taking birth control, counteracting the pill. Maybe a family member is nine months pregnant and jogging every day, but you are stuck on bed rest to have a healthy baby. Perhaps you have just had another miscarriage, and your best friend called to say she is expecting. Maybe you find an outfit that you purchased the day you found out you were pregnant.

Whatever the situation, grief can knock you down in a hurry. Usually, you are never prepared for it. Never ready for it, but wham, it is there in your face!!

It had been two years since Brayden passed when grief reared its ugly face. I ran into an old friend from high school while shopping one day. She let me know that she was expecting twins. I was ecstatic for her. I introduced my friend to her, and they exchanged pleasantries, congratulations were given, and we went on our way. A few days later, the friend who was with me called me. She worked at a funeral home, and she called to let me know that my high school friend was there. She had delivered her twins. One had survived, and the other had not. I was devasted but knew I had to go to her.

I never expected to see her child. I had not prepared myself for that. I walked into the funeral home, and there my friend was holding her precious daughter who had passed. My heart sank, and I wanted to run. I wanted to run so fast and far! I thought I could do this, but maybe it was too soon. She spotted me and approached me with her baby. I literally could not see anything because tears were pouring from my eyes. I wrapped her in my arms and wept with her. I looked at her beautiful sleeping angel and returned to the day I held Brayden in my arms.

This mama had no idea that inside I was dying! I was heartbroken for her, but it took me right back to that dark place. It took me back to the anger stage of grief. I wanted my son! I wanted him here! I should not know what this type of grief felt like; no one should! I did not want to be a part of this group of grieving moms. I wanted Brayden!

But then, as days and weeks went on and I talked to this mama more and more, I realized God put me in the right place at the right time. It was a Divine meeting that I saw her at Walmart that day *and* that I happened to have a friend with me who worked at the exact funeral home she would use a few days later who was also able to tell me she needed me. God knew!

It is okay when grief comes knocking at your door days, weeks, or years later! Give yourself the grace to go back. Time does not heal all wounds! Losing a child is like nothing I have ever experienced before! It has been twenty years since Brayden passed, and I still grieve. I grieve for what could have been. I grieve for what type of man he would be. I grieved when he turned sixteen and would be driving. I grieved the year he was supposed to graduate high school. You will repeat the stages of grief multiple times; the key is not to stay in those places. Keep placing one foot in front of the other. There is no time frame in which you must move to the next stage of grief, and DO NOT let anyone tell you there is.

Say His Name

September is still a hard month for me every year because I know I will celebrate yet another birthday at the cemetery at the end of the month. Sometimes we have family members that go with us, and sometimes it is just me, Justin, and our daughter. The day is always difficult, but we make it through. On his birthday, we always take purple roses, the Mourning Rose, for baby loss. I take the number of roses of how old Brayden would be, stuffed animals, cars or trucks, and always balloons to honor him each year.

When Brayden passed, we took many pictures of him. Not something I share with everyone, but in the beginning, I wanted people to see how beautiful he was. I was still a new mom and was proud of my baby. I quickly realized how uncomfortable it made some people feel to look at a deceased baby. Honestly, it never crossed my mind. They saw a deceased baby; I saw my precious son. Their reactions made me feel ashamed. I tucked the pictures away and dedicated a room in my house as my "angel" room, where I displayed all my keepsakes of Brayden.

I caught on quickly that people would not say his name. As if not mentioning his name would make me forget that he existed. Here is the truth, mothers who have lost babies want, no, we NEED people to remember our babies' names. They did exist! They are still a part of us. We want the recognition that they lived, even if we never met them. I have told mothers I have talked to after losing a baby by miscarriage to honor their baby with a name, piece of jewelry, or a tree planted in their honor. They lived! They were yours! It is okay to say their name!

As for me, I will always say my son's name. Brayden! Brayden is my son! I am a proud mom of a boy named Brayden!

Honor your child! Remember your child! However, that looks for you and your family. You will never replace that loss. Even if you have a hundred more children, you still have that one or two or three that your heart will always miss. Say their name! Do not let others make you feel ashamed of your child or what you have lost. Be proud of your baby!

Big Moves

I was desperate to re-establish some control over my life. Especially the few months after Brayden passed. I needed to change something in my life. Something big and scary that only I had control over. I had already made the decision that I could not go back to the house where all of our plans started while expecting to grow our family. Luckily, it was a rental, so I had that option. I felt completely out of control because I had no control over anything that happened to

Brayden. I wanted to move. I tried to get away from the town and the people. I needed a change of scenery. I called my dad, who lived three hundred miles from us, to ask if we could move in for a while. Without hesitation, he said yes.

We packed everything we had and put it in storage. We told our family and friends goodbye and headed East. We cried the entire time we were out of town. Not once did Justin refuse this significant change; he accepted that it was what I needed to heal. We pulled into a motel on our way because we were both so physically and emotionally exhausted, holding each other and crying the entire night. All I could think about was how I left Brayden behind. The cemetery was the only place I felt physically close to him.

We arrived in Fort Worth the following day. We were lost and had no clue what we were going to do, how to do it, or where to begin to do whatever it was. Justin started looking in the paper for jobs, while I quickly realized that this was a whim decision, possibly not the wisest thing I had done. But it felt so good to take control of something like a big move.

We packed all our things back up five days later and went home. Some say we never gave it a chance to work. Correct, we did not. It was not about making anything work as it was about control. I made a huge decision to move and control the uprooting of my life. Although it ended up being more like a vacation. That was okay with me. I said I was moving, and I did. Now I know, and I can go home. Somehow those five days made a huge difference for me and my mental health.

I will caution you, do not make crazy life-changing decisions on a whim. Sometimes you cannot go back. Sometimes those temporary solutions become a permanent fixture in your life. I suggest making changes that will encourage you. Volunteer work, grief counseling, talking to friends or family. Be careful; grief can be so tricky!

Broken Together

Although Justin and I had created and lost Brayden, our journeys were completely different in how we dealt with things. I was very vocal about my feelings, whereas Justin was the more "suffer in silence" type. We had no frame of reference on how to grieve together. We were both angry and did not know how to manage our emotions. I wanted him to be open with his feelings, and I think he wanted me to be silent.

I have been told and witnessed for myself that for parents who suffer baby loss, divorce rates increase, something no one tells you before you walk down the aisle. Let me say this, in no way was Justin taking anything out on me. He was kind and compassionate towards me always. But not once in my grief did I stop and ask him, "Are you okay?" I thought he was feeling everything I was feeling too.

Wow, was I ever wrong!

Years after losing Brayden, we went on a trip, turned off the radio in the car, and just talked. Justin opened up to me about what it was like for him to be alone with Brayden at the hospital. He told me how helpless he felt as our son grasped onto his finger as his little body slipped away. Justin told me how he sat for several moments before telling the nurse he did not know how to tell me that our son passed. He shared with me how he told the nurse she had to put baby lotion on Brayden before they brought him to me, because that was one of my favorite smells—a baby fresh out of a bath. He told me the hell he went through when we both woke up at four in the morning every day for a year after losing Brayden or how hard it was watching me wake up in a nightmare state because I dreamt I was still pregnant with Brayden.

I do not consider myself a selfish person, but I felt awful. Justin was so busy trying to keep me together that he fell apart himself. He knew I did not want to go back to that house, no problem. I wanted to move, no problem. I needed to sit and talk about Brayden, no problem. Inside he must have been screaming, "Stop, please stop!"

Justin coped by turning to drugs. I did not know of it at the time, but now I know it. It took him a year trying to keep me together. The next year it was his turn to fall apart, which ultimately led us to separate. I eventually filed for divorce. Thankfully, God had different plans.

We were broken together but so far apart. Yes, we lost the same baby, but he had no idea what I was feeling from a mom's point of view and vice versa. I had no idea what Justin was feeling from a father's perspective. Give your spouse much grace! Ask how they are doing. Listen to what they say. Let the man in your life break! They are dealing with loss too! Come together as a couple in unity as you extend understanding and unwavering love to each other. Hold one another up when one is down. No one can love that baby more than the two people who created him or her. 1 Corinthians 13:4-5 says, *"Love is patient, love is kind. It does not envy, it does not boast, it is not proud. It does not dishonor others, it is not self-seeing, it is not easily angered, it keeps no record of wrongs"* (NIV).

Forgiving Myself

I hated looking in the mirror. The only reflection I saw was that of a girl I used to know. I didn't recognize myself. I had not changed physically but mentally. I would never be the same; I had a scar on my body that reminded me of Brayden. But the scar inside that no one could see was much worse.

I could not let go of the fact that I did not know I was in labor. How could that happen? How did I "labor" all night long and not know it? I blamed myself. It was my fault

Brayden did not survive. Stupid girl! You call yourself a mom but could not fix what was wrong with him! Stupid girl! What did you do physically that caused this? Stupid girl! You are not even a whole woman! Stupid girl! You cannot have children! Stupid girl! Your husband will leave because you cannot give him children! Stupid girl!

EVERY DAY! I told myself these things every day! I told myself I was unworthy, unlovable, a useless woman. Until my family said, "You need counseling." I did not go to a grief counselor; I went to a pastor. Either type of counselor is fine as long as you get the healing you need. The pastor was wonderful for me. In the middle of the counseling session, he asked, "Why are you so mad?" I explained that I had brought this upon myself. It was my fault that I did not recognize the signs of labor. He began to weep. He said, "God does not work that way. Can you imagine a heaven where there are no children? Children bring us such joy. I cannot imagine heaven without them."

He got me thinking. Heaven sounds amazing while you are reading about it in the Bible. The one thing that excites me about heaven is seeing everyone who has gone before me. The Bible states in 1 Corinthians 13:12, *"We will be known as we were known."* Brayden will know that I am his mom! I will not have to wander the streets of gold looking for him; he will know me, I will know him! WOW! That excites me.

I slowly began to show myself some mercy. I was a first-time mom; I had no reference to labor, contractions, or anything else for that matter. I did NOT cause

Brayden's death! I ate healthily. I exercised! I did everything my doctor told me to do. I went through a mental checklist of pregnancy's do's and don'ts daily. It was not my fault. As mothers, we are supposed to be able to fix things, it is part of our nature, and I could not fix it. That is a hard pill to swallow.

Ladies, forgive yourself and your body. Forgive what you could not change. You would not choose to lose your baby. You found no pleasure in losing a part of you. Over time healing will come. Use your time to help other mothers as soon as you let go of the guilt you are not meant to carry. I have had friends with infertility issues who lose babies month after month. I cannot imagine the strength they have to keep trying or the guilt when they realize another loss has occurred. I think of Sarah in the Bible. She wanted a child for ninety years! Ninety years! God told her she would be the mother of nations (Genesis 17:16) I am sure Sarah had years of hatred against her own body. I am sure Sarah looked at her body with disgust. Forgive yourself and know that this is in no way your fault. Give yourself mercy and grace, then love who you are again.

Dreams

I have always been a believer in dreams. I believe God has given me dreams to prepare me for what is to come. My grandmother was a saint in my eyes. She passed away six months before I got married. I had dreams of her passing while Justin was in Army basic training. On a May morning, I received a phone call that my angel here on earth (my grandmother) had gone on to heaven.

I came to rely on dreams and tried to understand what the message was in them.

After losing Brayden, a friend that came into my life told me one day that she needed to tell me something. She dreamt that she was visiting Brayden's grave, and a woman walked up behind her, holding a little boy's hand. The woman said, "I need you to tell my Kindra something for me. Tell her she will have a baby when her little body is ready." The woman looked at the little boy and said, "Are you ready to go, Sunshine?"

Now, if you knew my grandmother, you would know that that is exactly how she spoke. Soft words, kind, gentle, and always thought of me as a baby. While I have an incredibly unique nickname that most people call me, my grandma called me her Sunshine. The other interesting fact about this dream is what direction she came from, which was from the direction of her grave. I had also placed chimes in the tree next to Brayden's grave the day before this dream, and my friend said she could hear chimes in the dream.

Of course, I asked all the questions. What did the woman look like, her hair and eyes? What was she wearing? What did the baby look like, his physical features? What was he wearing? I wanted all the details. The friend went with me to my mom's house, where my grandmother's picture hung on a wall. She went to the image and asked, "Who is this woman?" I told her it was my grandma. She said that was the woman in the dream. Wow! I see what you did there, God! I said many times that the only thing that comforted me in Brayden's passing was that he was with my grandma. I knew he was.

God gave me other dreams to follow through the years. He gave me the desire to go back to school to be an ultrasound technician. I told everyone I wanted to do this to help moms like myself. I hoped to hold the hand of a mother experiencing loss. The doors to that profession kept shutting in my face. I could not understand it until my best friend asked me what I thought about nursing. I had never really thought about it, but the doors swung wide open when I looked into it. I was accepted into a program the first time I applied.

My third semester of school included pediatric and OB classes. I was doing my clinical on labor and delivery when a young pregnant lady came in saying she thought her water had broken. She was twenty-two weeks along, her first pregnancy carrying a baby girl, and full of hope. The room was very heavy when the nurse discovered that her water had broken. My heart went out to this young mom because we knew the outcome would not be good. Medically babies cannot survive in the womb without the amniotic fluid.

After completing my rotation, I stayed to sit with this mom for a few extra minutes. I sat on her bed, held her hand, and assured her this was not her fault. There was nothing she did to cause this or anything she could have done to prevent this. I told her that her darkest days would be the next few days, weeks, and months to come. I prayed with her and her family. I wanted her to know she was not alone. She was not the first person to go through this enormous loss; sadly, she would not be the last.

At that moment, I knew what God wanted me to do. He wanted me to work with mothers who had suffered a loss. I still have no idea what the entire picture looks like for me, but I feel my purpose is to help those enduring the pain that comes from loss.

Rainbow Babies

I was in no rush to have another baby.
I was absolutely terrified of being pregnant.
The thought of going through another loss
was a paralyzing fear for me. But that stick yet
again had a plus sign on it. Was I ready? I did
not know.

I will say that I feel guilty over this
now, but when I was pregnant with my
daughter, Destiny, I did not do all the things I
did with Brayden. I did not read or sing as
much. The fear of becoming attached to her

was paralyzing for me. When I discovered I was pregnant with our daughter, the only comfort I felt came from the dream my friend shared with the message from my grandma.

I had a cerclage put into my cervix twelve weeks into my pregnancy, which helped to prevent the cervix from dilating. At twenty-two weeks pregnant, I started feeling those "active" motions I had with Brayden. I immediately went to the hospital and learned I was dilating again. Luckily, I had only dilated two centimeters. I was put on bed rest for twelve weeks. People ask, "How did you do that?" My response never changes, "Celebrate a birthday at the cemetery once and tell me what you will not do for your child."

Our sweet rainbow baby was born six weeks early but was healthy. We knew the perfect name for her was Destiny. She was like my salvation when she was born. For the second time in my life, I knew what pure love felt like. I often joke that Brayden would have been a very pretty boy because I saw so many similarities in them. We have always shared Brayden's story with Destiny. She finds comfort in going to the cemetery and being near him. She has what others describe as a strange "connection" to him, but it is simply a sibling's love to me. She did have an "imaginary" friend for a bit, named Sweetheart. Her friend was a boy that she described as looking like herself. I know some find that things like this are hard to believe, I was skeptical, but I believe God sends signs of comfort.

I would often be asked when I was having the next baby. I have never understood why people ask these things. They have no idea the internal struggle you deal with after losing a baby, with the physical and emotional toll it takes on your body and mind. I feel abundantly blessed to have my healthy daughter. I have something that some people only hope and pray for after losing a baby. I thought I had to prove that I was woman enough to carry a child. I realized quickly that I did not! God had already blessed me more than I deserved being the mom of these two beautiful humans.

I understand that not everyone gets to have a happy ending with a rainbow baby. I am not naïve. I do not know what everyone's journey looks like in their healing process. Perhaps your journey is repeated IVF to have your baby finally. Surrogacy is a beautiful solution for many. Adoption is a way to love a child because their birth moms wanted something different for them. Foster parenting is an avenue to spread your love to many children in need. Some are blessed to be a "stepmom" or bonus mom, as I like to say, and can share the love of their spouse's children. Maybe you are the favorite aunt to nieces and nephews. There are many types of moms. I do not believe that you are only a mom when you carry a child. Spread your mama love!

The Language of Tears

Remember when I said I wanted no part in the "tear language" with God? I honestly had no choice in that. There were days that crying was all I did. I realized that God had not done this *to* me. He did not make my body imperfect. He was not punishing me for something I prayed about or didn't. It did not take God by surprise when a boy named Brayden was born on that September day.

I have shed so many tears for Brayden. Tears are a liquid prayer. I may not speak anything verbally as the tears flow from my eyes, but God knows. God knows each time I spill a tear where that hurt comes from in my heart. Just as God watched the tears flow from Jesus, He kept every tear. I stopped being angry with God when I realized he knew what I had gone through. He lost a son too. But if He knows every sparrow falling from a tree, how much more does he love Brayden or me!

Prayer is our love language with God. Just as a parent watching their child throw a temper tantrum, God watched me throw mine. His patience never faltered. He opened his arms to me after I finished throwing a fit and quieted my heart and spirit. He gave me peace that passes all understanding. I cannot explain my push and pull game with God and why it went on for so long. I wanted to be angry with Him but cried out daily for strength. I realized in quiet moments that all I had to do was whisper "Jesus," and I felt His comfort again.

Joy Comes in the Morning

I was afraid to be happy again. I wanted to be sad. I felt that if I found joy, I was somehow betraying Brayden. But with any loss, life goes on. I was forever changed when Brayden passed away. I honestly think of him daily as if he is still here.

In my journey, I have learned some essential life lessons. I learned that the desire to have a baby differs from the need to be a mother. I believe it is a maternal gift that God gives women, even if you are unaware of having such a desire. I wanted to get woken up in the middle of the night by a newborn crying. I desired to be sleep deprived to take care of my baby. I wanted to change dirty diapers. I wanted to be a mother in every sense of the word.

I learned that twenty years later, the pain is still fresh. I cannot come to say the word "died" when talking about Brayden. I still say, "passed away or lost." As though I misplaced him somewhere. I do not know what it is about that word that makes it sound scary or permanent.

I learned that people could be cruel and toxic regarding your loss. I experienced this firsthand from a family member. I was told that this was my fault. Now, as many of you know, we already blame ourselves. We blame ourselves because, again, we cannot fix it. We cannot change it. I had someone tell me that if I had taken better care of myself, I would not have experienced this pain. As sick as it is, I believed them. I had someone verbalize what I was feeling inside. It was almost a relief to have someone say it. Sick, I know. I now know that was not the case. I do not believe God works that way. God is not a vengeful God who punishes us through things like this. But I carried this for a long while and still sometimes question if they were right. Please know that I have forgiven this person through lots of prayers. No matter what type of loss you are dealing with, this is not your fault.

I have learned that God will give me joy again. It may not come in the form of another child. It may not come soon. I know that if tears could be a river to heaven, I would have been able to see Brayden every day. God has blessed and used me to share my testimony with other ladies. I think of the verse about weeping endures through the night, but joy comes in the morning. I am no longer a mom of mourning; I am a mom of morning. I accept my joy. I receive the new grace given each morning. I no longer feel severe pain in the memory of Brayden; I feel the joy of being his mom. I have the six months of my pregnancy that I think of fondly. I think of that precious cry and feel the joy that I heard it. I think of Justin's short but beautiful hours with Brayden alone. I think of that beautiful face I tried to memorize. I look at my daughter and thank God that she is here, and I can love her with no guilt.

Embrace each part of this incredible journey. We are MOMs, moms of the morning. We accept our joy after a season of grief and our testimony through our biggest test. Psalm 30:5 says, *"For his anger endureth but a moment, in his favour is life: weeping may endure for a night, but joy cometh in the morning."*

About the Author

Kindra King is a 42-year-old wife, mother, and Registered Nurse. who has been married to her high school sweetheart for 21 years. She has worked in Pediatrics and Hospice settings as a nurse.

In her spare time, she loves to read, sing, have family game nights, and attend concerts. She is also passionate about people and loves to hear their stories.

Visit www.kindraking.com for more information or email her at:
authorkindraking@gmail.com.